TALMUD
WITH TRAINING WHEELS

Courtyards and Classrooms: Bava Batra 20b–22a

JOEL LURIE GRISHAVER

Credits

Cover: © David Kreider (www.kreiderart.com) ■ Pages 6: © Robert Holmes/CORBIS Page 7: © Michael S. Yamashita/CORBIS Page 10: © Catherine Jennings ■ Page 11: © Israel Ministry of Tourism ■ Page 25: Royalty Free/CORBIS ■ Page 27: © Henry Diltz/CORBIS ■ Pages 28: © Shai Ginott/CORBIS ■ Pages 36/37/39: © Jack Hazut

ISBN #1-891662-30-9

Copyright © 2003
Joel Lurie Grishaver

Torah Aura Productions, 4423 Fruitland Avenue, Los Angeles, CA 90058
(800) BE-TORAH • (800) 238-6724 • (323) 585-7312 • fax (323) 585-0327
Website WWW.TORAHAURA.COM

MANUFACTURED IN CHINA

Table of Contents

The INTRODUCTION

Bava Batra

This text comes from the second chapter of the tractate **Bava Batra** (the Third Gate). It is in the section of the Talmud called *Nezikin,* which means "damages," but in law school it would be called "torts." In *Nezikin* are three books called "the gates": *Bava Kamma* (the First Gate), *Bava Metzia* (the Middle Gate) and *Bava Batra* (the Third or Final Gate). In ancient Israel the elders would sit in the gates of the city and "judge between the people." I have always felt—without any textual proof—that the word *Bava*, gate, recalls those times.

Talmud pages have two sides, "a" and "b." This is because they were originally printed one side per page at a time and then sewn together. Numbering pages with individual numbers started when printers learned how to print eight-page folios and they needed the individual numbers to know how to fold and cut the pages the right way. This text starts on the second side of page 20 and goes to the first side of page 22.

Hazakah

In the first chapter of **Bava Batra** we are introduced to a legal principle called **HAZAKAH**. HAZAKAH comes from the Hebrew word HAZAK, which means "strong." It relates to the kind of "pull" that someone has (due to time invested) that can allow him or her to force a situation in his or her own favor. In this SUGIA (Talmudic dialogue) we are going to deal with two extensions of HAZAKAH, one educational and one commercial.

- In education, HAZAKAH is very much like what we call tenure. By virtue of teaching so many years, a teacher is granted job security regardless of the competitive qualities of other teachers.

- HAZAKAH also applies to business. In commerce, a business that has HAZAKAH may be granted exclusivity through "zoning" because of the time invested.

Hasagat Gevul

In the second half of this SUGIA the idea of HAZAKAH grows into another concept called HASAGAT GEVUL—the infringement of boundaries.

In the Torah we are told:

A LARGE, DARK STONE MARKS THE BORDER BETWEEN SCOTLAND AND ENGLAND.

> Deut. 19.14: You shall not erase your neighbor's boundary marker that they have set in your collective inheritance in the Land that God gave you to inherit.

This is echoed in a second verse:

> Deut. 27.17: Cursed be anyone who moves a neighbor's boundary marker.

These two verses are talking about the theft of property through the altering of boundaries. A thief can enlarge a holding through moving or removing a marker and scarfing up property that belonged to a neighbor. The commentators notice that the first verse is clearly talking about the Land of Israel but use the second verse (that doesn't refer to Israel) to generalize the value.

> Rashi[1]: Planting a tree near the boundary of a property may be a violation of HASAGAT GEVUL because the roots may steal water and nutrition from a neighbor's property. (on Shabbat 85b)

> Tosafot[2]: Quoting words from another Torah teacher or student without giving credit can be seen as an infringement on another person's property.

And in this SUGIA this principle is expanded to cover economic situations, too.

Baraita: **Other fishermen's nets must be kept away from the hiding spot of a fish that has already been spotted by another fisherman. They must be kept as far away as the distance that a fish normally swims, just under three miles.**

Amora 1: Even though the fish are not yet in the net, they are essentially already caught. By fishing in the first fisherman's zone you are essentially stealing the fish he is certain to catch.

[1]**RASHI.** Rabbi Shlomo Yitzhaki. 1040–1105. French biblical and Talmudic commentator. Rashi is "the" commentator on the Bible and on the Talmud. He received his early Talmudic training in his native Troyes, France, before traveling to Mainz and Worms (Germany), and returned to Troyes at the age of twenty-five as one of the leading Talmudists of his day. He taught and wrote while earning his livelihood as a wine merchant. Rashi spent most of his life on his Talmud commentary. Rashi gathered around him a number of key students and studied with them daily. His commentaries grew out of their regular study sessions. His commentaries provide the foundation on which most other Jewish commentary is based. He marked the trail others follow through this material. His later years were marred by the excruciating suffering of the Jews during the First Crusade in 1096, when many important Jewish communities were destroyed.

[2]**Tosafot** (meaning "the additions"). A set of critical notes that run parallel to Rashi, made up of more than forty-three identifiable voices. They clearly begin as the additions made by Rashi's actual students and grow through the voices of his students' students.

WARMUP: Case Studies

Before you begin this Talmudic text, get yourself into the right context by working out your best solution to the following cases. We will look at their resolution at the end of this passage.

1. CAPITAL BASEBALL: The Montreal Expos is a failing Major League Baseball franchise. On any given night minor league teams in Akron, Toledo and Kalamazoo draw more fans. The Expos' stadium, Stade Olympique (Olympic Stadium), is decrepit, obsolete, and even dangerous. The owners are considering moving the franchise. Washington, D.C., seems to be the best possible location. The city has a large and diverse population, plenty of wealthy corporations and individuals who would buy season tickets and luxury boxes, and a fan base spanning two states (Virginia and Maryland) and the District. A group of investors wants to build a new stadium in D.C.'s Virginia suburbs and lure the Expos from Montreal.

The problem is Peter Angelos, who owns the nearby Baltimore Orioles. Major League Baseball is exempt from federal anti-trust laws. The Orioles are currently, in practical terms, Washington D.C.'s team. Since the Washington Senators left thirty years ago, the Orioles are the closest team to the nation's capital. Angelos is worried that a new team in the Washington area would prevent the Orioles from attracting fans from the D.C. area (especially fans with the money to afford season tickets and luxury boxes). He says that a team in Washington would infringe on his property. (This case was current when we were publishing this book.)

YOU BE THE JUDGE: Should a baseball team owner in Baltimore have the right to stop the opening of a baseball franchise in the Washington, D.C. area?

References: Virginia Baseball Stadium Authority FAQ: www.baseballinva.org/faqs.asp?SIT=View#; the Baltimore Orioles: http://baltimore.orioles.mlb.com

2. TAX COLLECTORS: Simon leases the right to collect taxes from a feudal lord. He pays the lord a fee and keeps all of the taxes he collects. Reuben comes and offers the feudal lord a higher fee to collect taxes in the same district. Simon will lose his "job" as the tax collector and his way of earning a living (*She'elot u'Teshuvot Maharshal* # 89[3]).

YOU BE THE JUDGE: Should Reuben be forced to withdraw his higher offer?

3. HIGH FASHION: There is a street in the city that is the center of women's fashion. Here many designers have boutiques. Susan wants to become a designer and open her own boutique. She goes to rent a vacant store, but when Valerie, who already has a store in the same building, finds out, she tells her landlord not to rent to another women's clothing store. The landlord, who is worried about losing a tenant, refuses to rent to Susan.

YOU BE THE JUDGE: Should the landlord be forced to grant Susan a lease? Did Valerie do a reasonable thing?

4. MISHNEH TORAH COMPETITION: This is a real and famous

case about copyright. Rabbi Meir of Padua edited a corrected version of Maimonides' *Mishneh Torah* and published it in partnership with Aloizi Brogodin of Venice. Marcos Antonio, another publisher from Venice, put out his own competitive edition of the *Mishneh Torah* and sold it a cheaper price. Rabbi Meir went to a local rabbinical court and asked them to forbid the competitive edition because it would destroy his entire investment (*Rama, Responsa* 10[4]).

YOU BE THE JUDGE: Should Marcos Antonio be stopped from selling his edition of the Mishneh Torah?

5. NEW SHUL: In an older part of the city that used to be the Jewish neighborhood, an old synagogue is barely staying above water. It does not really have enough members to pay its monthly costs, and it barely gets a minyan. This synagogue is run by the old-timers and is not very hip. A group of younger Jews in the community, some of whom have previously joined the old synagogue but many of whom did not, decide to open a synagogue of their own—one that would better serve their spiritual and social needs. The new group tries to rent a storefront. The old group goes to a *Bet Din* (rabbinical court) to block the rental on the grounds that the new synagogue will put the old one out of business.

YOU BE THE JUDGE: Should the new synagogue be prevented from getting off the ground (*Iggerot Moshe, Ḥosen Mishpat* #38[5])?

[3]**THE MAHARSHAL.** Solomon Ben Yeḥiel Luria. 1510–1574. Polish legal authority and Talmudic commentator. He wrote the *Yam Shel Shlomo* and a commentary on the *Shulḥan Arukh*.

[4]**RAMA.** Moses ben Israel Isserles. 1525–1572. Polish legal scholar. He was the great-grandson of Yehiel Luria, the first rabbi of Brisk, studied in Lublin, and founded a yeshiva in Cracow. His best-known work was the *Mappa* (the Tablecloth), a commentary on the *Shulḥan Arukh* (the Set Table), written by Yosef Caro. The *Shulḥan Arukh* focuses on Sephardic customs while the *Mappa* emphasizes Ashkenazic tradition.

[5]**RABBI MOSHE FEINSTEIN.** 1895–1986. American Talmudic authority and legal decisor. Born in Uzda, near Minsk, Belorussia, he came to the United States in 1937 and became the Rosh Yeshiva (dean) of Metivta Tiferet Yerushalayim, a yeshiva in New York. His halakhic decisions have been published in a collection, *Iggerot Moshe* (The Letters of Moshe).

TALMUDIC ZONING

This Talmudic passage will concern itself with the difference in zoning between three different kinds of space. When most of the Families-of-Israel lived on farms, privacy was not a problem, but once they began living in cities, figuring out how to share living space became a serious issue. The Talmud created three levels of space: the courtyard, the alley and the marketplace.

HATZER: Courtyard

A courtyard is a fenced or walled area that belongs to one or more houses. If it belongs to one house, it is part of the private space that belongs to that house. This is the replication of the farm in the city. The courtyard is more or less the urban version of the farmyard.

If a courtyard is shared by two or more houses, it is shared private space. City families had to figure out how to create a frontyard or backyard that allowed families to have a sense of protection and privacy from the larger population while still accommodating the neighbors who shared that space.

Often the oven was placed in the courtyard (to avoid "baking" the people who lived on the second floor). If one wanted to carry food from the oven into the house on Shabbat, one had to turn a courtyard into a single area. One is not allowed to carry from inside to outside or outside to inside on Shabbat unless it is a single area. If the courtyard is gated with at least a beam across the entrance, it is considered a single area, and one can then carry.

The first part of this passage will deal with the issues of setting up businesses in "shared private space."

MAVOI: Alley

A MAVOI is an alley off of which branch several HATZEROT (courtyards). This MAVOI is a corridor between the HATZER and the street (RESHUT ha-RABIM/public space). A MAVOI is both physically and legally halfway between a street and a courtyard.

Often, in mishnaic times, a house would have its own courtyard, while many such houses would share a single MAVOI as common space.

One is allowed to carry objects on Shabbat in a <u>H</u>ATZER, but one is not allowed to do so in RESHUT ha-RABIM/public space. If a MAVOI has a crossbeam that separates it from the street, and one has an arrangement that involves sharing food among residents (ERUV TAVSHILIM), one is able to carry within an alley on Shabbat.

In the second half of this passage we will examine the similarities and differences involved in opening a business in a MAVOI as compared to a <u>H</u>ATZER. We will be asking this: How private is a MAVOI?

SHUK: Marketplace

The SHUK is the bazaar. This is the public marketplace where anyone can come and do business. The SHUK (which is RESHUT ha-RABIM/public space) is the "main street" of the rabbinic city.

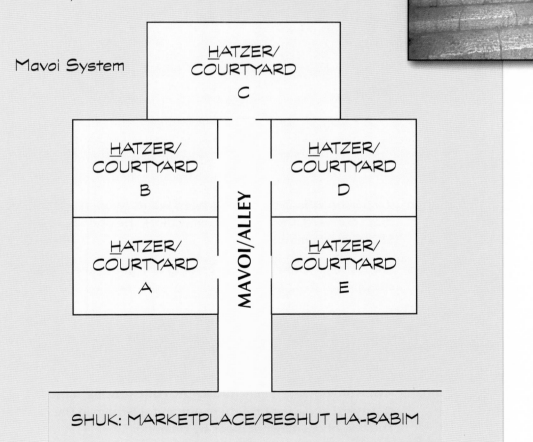

Mavoi System

	HATZER/ COURTYARD C	
HATZER/ COURTYARD B	MAVOI/ALLEY	HATZER/ COURTYARD D
HATZER/ COURTYARD A		HATZER/ COURTYARD E

SHUK: MARKETPLACE/RESHUT HA-RABIM

The Mishnah: Bava Batra 2.3

חֲנוּת שֶׁבֶּחָצֵר, יָכוֹל לִמְחוֹת בְּיָדוֹ וְלוֹמַר
לוֹ אֵינִי יָכוֹל לִישֹׁן,
מִקּוֹל הַנִּכְנָסִין וּמִקּוֹל הַיּוֹצְאָין.
אֲבָל עוֹשֶׂה כֵלִים, יוֹצֵא וּמוֹכֵר בְּתוֹךְ הַשּׁוּק,
אֲבָל אֵינוֹ יָכוֹל לִמְחוֹת בְּיָדוֹ
וְלוֹמַר לוֹ אֵינִי יָכוֹל לִישֹׁן
לֹא מִקּוֹל הַפַּטִּישׁ,
וְלֹא מִקּוֹל הָרֵחַיִם,
וְלֹא מִקּוֹל הַתִּינוֹקוֹת:

Narrator: [REYSHA—The First Case]

Gris: "REYSHA" is an Aramaic version of the word
ראֹשׁ "ROSH" (as in "Rosh ha-Shanah").
Rosh means "head." The "ah" ending is an
extra א. An א at the end of a word is an
Aramaic way of saying "the" (like a הַ at the
start of a Hebrew word).

Mishnah: If a person who lives in a courtyard wants to open a STORE in that courtyard, the neighbors may block the opening of the STORE by claiming:

Neighbors: The noise of your customers coming and going keeps me from sleeping.

Narrator: [SEYFA—The Second Case]

Gris: "SEYFA" comes from the Hebrew word סוֹף "SOF," meaning "end." The "ah" ending is another א that means "the."

Mishnah: A person, however, may MANUFACTURE articles in the courtyard and then take them out and sell them in the market. The neighbors may not block by claiming:

TYPOGRAPHICAL KEY
This is the way type fonts are used in this translation.

Biblical Text

TANNA'ITIC MATERIAL: a mishnah or a baraita

AMORA'IC MATERIAL: Commentaries written during the time of the Gemara

RASHI & Friends: Anything in this type comes from the commentators.

JOEL LURIE GRISHAVER's additions to the text.

Neighbors: [1] The noise of the hammer keeps me from sleeping.

[2] The noise of the millstones keeps me from sleeping.

Narrator: or

Neighbors: [3] The noise of children keeps me from sleeping.

Gris: *"One of these things is not like the other." The commentators notice that the "noise of children" doesn't seem connected to manufacturing the same way as are "the noise of the hammer" and "the noise of the millstone." They assume that there must be a logic to the Mishnah's clustering of these elements, and so they work to come up with theories about the connection.*

Bartinura[6]: What does "our Mishnah" mean by "the noise of children"? It means the noise made by the children who come to shop at the stores.

Ramban[7]: Here is another way of understanding "our MISHNAH": The "NOISE" is not really the issue, and the "VOLUME of SOUND" gives no neighbor the right to block a business. What the Mishnah is really talking about is the right of a neighbor to object to the TRAFFIC created by people coming in and out of his or her living space. In our Mishnah, "NOISE" means the "BUSY-NESS" of the business. It is a privacy issue.

Gris: *If The Bartinura is right, we are talking about corner shops that just serve local children who are allowed to enter a courtyard to shop because it is safer than allowing them out on the larger street. If the Ramban is right, the children are "local," resident children and are part of the backdrop anyway.*

[6]**THE BARTINURA.** Rabbi Ovadiah Yarel from the Italian city of Bertinoro. 1440–1518. Mishnah commentator. When you are studying just Mishnah (without the Gemara) you turn to him to guide you. Rabbi Ovadiah draws from the commentaries of Rashi on the Gemara, and Rambam on the Mishnah. His abbreviation is "the Rav." The commentary he wrote on the Mishnah was finished in *Eretz Yisrael* about 1500.

[7]**RAMBAN.** Rabbi Moshe Ben Nahman (Nahmanides). 1194-1270. Biblical and Talmudic commentator, Kabbalist and poet. In 1263 Ramban was ordered by King James of Aragon to hold a religious disputation with a Jewish apostate, Pablo Christiani, at Barcelona. Ramban won and was rewarded by King James with a gift of three hundred coins. The fanatical Dominicans, however, began spreading the rumor that their side had won the debate. Ramban published an exact account of the questions and answers from the debate, *Sefer ha-Vikuah,* but the Dominicans presented only selected passages to the king, who had him expelled from Aragon.

13

The Gemara: Bava Batra 20b–22a

ACT I: Noisy Courtyards & Out-of-control Classrooms

Scene 1: The Basic Debate—Abaye vs. Rava on "The Noise of Children"

Narrator: The rabbis begin their discussion of "our Mishnah" by assuming that "the NOISE of CHILDREN" mentioned at the end of the Mishnah refers to "the NOISE of CHILDREN acting as customers."

(This assumption will later be challenged, but this is their starting point.) They ask:

Amora 1[8]: Why is the rule in the SEYFA (Part II) that says that neighbors can't complain about the noise of children visiting stores different from the rule in the REYSHA (Part I) where neighbors can complain about the noise made by other (adult) customers? What makes the noise made by adult customers forbidden and the noise made by child customers acceptable?

Narrator: Abaye and Rava were academic rivals. They present conflicting explanations.

Abaye[9]: Here is my theory. When the SEYFA says "THE NOISE OF CHILDREN" it actually means "THE NOISE OF CHILDREN OR ANY OTHER CUSTOMERS" visiting a business in a neighboring courtyard. If this is so, the Mishnah is teaching that you don't have the right to block a business (on account of noise) in a space where you don't reside.

GRIS: This opinion is not as outrageous as it sounds. Abaye is not going out of his way to "read into" this text. For the rabbis, the text of the Mishnah is a lot like lecture notes that were taken by someone else. They are filled with shorthand and are assumed to be more a memory device than a complete text. Therefore, Abaye is making his best guess at how to expand this brief note about NOISE.

Narrator: Rava said to him:

14

Rava[10]: Wrong! If you were right and this is what the Mishnah meant, it would have directly said, "It is permitted to open a store in another courtyard, and only the people who live in that courtyard can block it."

Narrator: Rather, Rava taught:

Rava: Here is my theory. The SEYFA of this Mishnah is actually talking about the noise made by schoolchildren from elsewhere coming into a courtyard (as customers do) to study Torah. The Mishnah's ruling came after the TIKKUN (reform) of Yehoshua ben Gamla.

Gris: TIKKUN means "to repair" or "to fix." That is its meaning in "TIKKUN OLAM," which means "fixing the world." Here a "TIKKUN" is an ordinance that corrects a problem situation.

Scene 2: Yehoshua ben Gamla and the History of Jewish Education

Narrator: The Gemara now goes on to provide historical background for the TIKKUN of Yehoshua ben Gamla.

Narrator: Rabbi Judah taught us that Rav taught him this history lesson:

Rav[11]: The name of the man who is to be blessed is Yehoshua ben Gamla[12]. Were it not for him, the Jewish people would have lost the Torah.

[Phase 1] In the beginning, every son was taught by his own father. If a boy had no father, he did not learn.

Gris: Formal Jewish education in the Rabbinic Era was only for boys. There is nothing we can do about that. The positive side of the story is that it was universal and paid for by the community.

The Gemara now asks the first of its two questions about a teaching: "Do you have a source for this?" (See "The Two Questions" in the introductory volume.)

Amora 1: Where in the Torah did they learn this practice?

Amora 2: They learned this practice from Deuteronomy 11.19:

Torah: וְלִמַּדְתֶּם אֹתָם אֶת־בְּנֵיכֶם

And you shall teach them to your children...

Amora 2: This practice emphasized the word:

Torah: אֹתָם [OTAM] "Your."

[8]**AMORA:** A technical term for the rabbis whose studies produced the Gemara. Amora means "a speaker."

[9]**ABAYE.** 278–338 C.E. Babylonian Amora. An orphan who was adopted by his uncle, Rabbah bar Naḥmani (a.k.a Rabbah), became the head of the yeshiva at Pumbedita after the death of Rabbi Yosef. He was a farmer as well as a scholar who is reported to have irrigated his fields at night so that he could study during the day. Abaye's regular rival was Rava. Their arguments and discussions form the core of much of the Talmud. It was during the time of Rava and Abaye that the Babylonian scholars made the final break with *Eretz Yisrael* and began what became the Babylonian Talmud.

[10]**RAVA.** Rava ben Yosef ben Hama. Babylonian Amora. 280–352 C.E. He studied in Sura under Rabbi Ḥisda and became a friend of Rami ben Ḥama. Then he went to Pumbedita and studied under Rabbah bar Naḥamani along with Abaye. When Abaye was picked to succeed their teacher, Rava established his own school in Maḥoza.

[11]**RAV.** Babylonian Amora. 200s C.E. Rav was part of the bridge beween the Mishnah and the Gemara, the Tannaim and the Amora'im, Eretz Yisrael and Babylon. A student of Yehudah Ha-Nasi, he was born in Babylonia but studied in Eretz Yisrael. He was appointed a market commissioner by the Exilarch. When he refused to ignore Palestinian practice and regulate prices, he was forced to leave his job. He went to Sura where he established a school and attracted hundreds of students. Rav is sometimes considered to be a Tanna.

[12]**YEHOSHUA BEN GAMLA:** *Kohein Ha-Gadol* (High Priest). Just before 70 C.E. During the last rebellion he opposed the war and was removed from office by Agrippa II. He remained a member of the Great Sanhedrin.

Amora 2:   In the Torah the word אֹתָם [O-TAM] is written without a ו VAV and can also be read as אַתֶּם [ATEM]. When you do that, the translation of וְלִמַּדְתֶּם אַתֶּם אֶת־בְּנֵיכֶם [V'LIMMADITEM ATEM ET B'NAIKHEM] becomes:

Torah: And you, *yourself*, shall teach them...

Rav: [Phase 2] When this practice proved ineffective because it left out lots of children who did not have fathers who could do the job, the TANNA'IM (the rabbis of the Mishnah) ruled that teachers of young children should be appointed in Jerusalem so that any young person could go there and learn.

Amora 1:   Where in the Torah did they root this new practice?

Rava: They evolved it from the words of the prophet Isaiah (2.3):

Isaiah[13]:   כִּי מִצִּיּוֹן תֵּצֵא תוֹרָה וּדְבַר־יהוה מִירוּשָׁלָם

From Zion shall go forth the Torah and the word of the Eternal from Jerusalem.

Tosafot: Why Jerusalem? The environment of Jerusalem particularly supported Torah study—it was like something in the air. When a person saw the Holiness of the Temple and the kind of Holy Work the Kohanim did, he was inspired to point his heart toward the awe of God and the study of Torah.

Rav: When this was put into practice, there was still a problem. If a child had a father, the father would take him up to Jerusalem and have him taught there. But if he did not have a father, he would not go up and learn.

[Phase 3] The TANNA'IM therefore ruled that teachers should be appointed in each PREFECTURE (Roman administrative district) and that boys should enter school at the age of sixteen or seventeen.

But this still didn't work well because when teachers tried to discipline students that old, the students would rebel and then leave school.

Rivta[14]:   Why did they choose sixteen or seventeen? That seems foolish. The practice taught in the Mishnah, according to Pirke Avot 5.21, is that five or six is the right age to begin schooling. The problem was this: when there was only a district school, it was considered too difficult and too dangerous for younger students to travel to another town.

Rav: [Phase 4] This is when Yehoshua ben Gamla ruled:

Yehoshua b. Gamla: Teachers of young children should be appointed in each district and each town. This makes it possible for children to enter school at the age of six or seven.

Narrator: And this history explains why many courtyards were locations where teachers held scheduled classes—creating the problem suggested as belonging to OUR MISHNAH. Each city and village now had its own small school, often in the house of a local teacher.

The Talmud now continues on this tangent by sharing some teaching tips. Eventually we will get back to the debate about businesses in a courtyard.

Scene 3: A Tangent—Rav's Thoughts about Jewish Teaching

Narrator: As long as we have been reviewing Rav's lesson on "The History of Jewish Education," we will take a minute and learn three famous teaching tips from Rav.

Rav said to RABBI SHMUEL BEN SHILAT[15]:

Rav: [TIP 1] Do not accept students younger than six. You can accept them after that and stuff them with Torah like an ox.

Rashi: This means that just as you can fatten an ox against its will, so you can "stuff Torah" into a not-so-willing student.

Narrator: Rav also said to Rabbi Shmuel ben Shilat:

Rav: [TIP 2] When you punish a child, hit him only with a shoelace.

Rashi: This is a metaphor that means "Do not eject a student from the class or punish that student excessively." In other words, "Don't use the whip."

Rav: [TIP 3] A good student will motivate himself. Place a distracted student next to a successful one and let him be company for his friends.

Rashi: This means that eventually the good students will provide the problem student with an example and with motivation.

Maharsha[16]: I think you have the pronouns backwards. I think it has the opposite meaning. The distracted student should stay in class and provide company for his friends, the good students, lest they decide to leave with him—or think they might have more fun out of class.

[13]**ISAIAH.** Prophet. Late 700s/early 600s B.C.E. The Book of Isaiah is made up of 66 chapters and looks like a single work. Chapters 1–39 of the Book of Isaiah are from the time when Assyria was conquering the Jewish people of the Northern Kingdom. Chapters 40–55 concern the period of the Exile in Babylonia, which started in 586 B.C.E. and affected all the Jews in Israel. The last chapters deal with the post-exilic period, when the Jewish people were re-establishing Zion, or Israel, and building themselves once again into a prosperous nation. Isaiah may be a composite of three or more people.

[14]**THE RITVA.** Rabbi Yom Tov Ibn Avraham Asevilli. 1250–1330. Spanish Talmudic commentator and Kabbalist. He was a student of the Rashba.

[15]**RABBI SHMUEL BEN SHILAT.** Babylonian Amora. First half of third century C.E. He was a student of Rav's whose major focus was teaching children. Once Rav found him standing in his own garden during school hours and asked him why he was there. Shmuel answered, "For thirteen years I have not seen my garden, and even now my thoughts are of pupils." Whereupon Rav applied to him the verse (Dan. 12:3), "They that turn the many to righteousness [shall shine] as the stars for ever and ever" (BB 8b).

[16]**MAHARSHA** is the acronym for Morenu Ha-Rav Shemu'el Adels, who lived in Ostog, Poland, 1555–1631. He is the author of a pair of books that are included in almost every edition of the Talmud. One was called *Halakhic Innovations;* the other was called *Aggadic Innovations.*

Scene 4: A Return to the Debate—Testing Rava's Opinion

Narrator: Now we return to Rava's interpretation of our Mishnah—that "The NOISE OF THE CHILDREN" means "the noise of children going to school."

GRIS: The AMORA'IM (the rabbis of the Gemara) come to the Gemara's second question. Having found a "biblical source" for this practice, we move on to: "Does anyone know any contradictions?" The AMORA'IM will use this question two ways. (1) First they will check out the validity of Rava's reasoning by making sure that it is consistent with all other accepted pieces of the "Oral Torah." (2) In the process of analyzing the possible contradictions, we will learn more about our topic. To do this, the text will introduce a series of BERAITOT. A BARAITA is a piece of material from the time of the Mishnah, from rabbis quoted in the Mishnah, that was not chosen to be part of the Mishnah. (See "The Two Questions" in the introductory volume.)

Narrator: One rabbi who is not named disagrees with Rava's explanation that the noise of children refers to noise of children in school that should be permitted. He quotes a BARAITA.

Amora 2: I think you're wrong, because this Baraita contradicts your explanation. It bans the teaching of children in a courtyard.

Baraita 1[17]: **If the resident of a courtyard wishes to open a business as (1) a mohel, (2) a blood-letter, (3) a weaver or (4) a teacher of children in his house, the other residents can block him.**

Rava: Your BARAITA doesn't prove anything. It doesn't mention Torah teaching. It refers to a teacher of "OVEID KOKHAVIM" (pagan children) not a teacher of Torah. So since Yehoshua ben Gamla orders it, Hebrew school can still be held in courtyards.

Rashba[18] & Ritva: The Gemara says "pagan," but it means any teaching but Torah. It was teaching that we make a zoning exemption for Torah learning and nothing else. It assumed that if they were Jewish kids, it would be Torah.

Tosafot: So what is wrong with the weaver working in the courtyard? Isn't the weaver doing manufacturing that is allowed in a courtyard and cannot be blocked? Yes, but this refers to a weaver who works for others, has customers and doesn't personally go out and sell his work to the public.

Narrator: Then the rabbi who is arguing with Rava quotes a second Baraita.

Tanna 2[19]: Then maybe this Baraita will *convince* you.

Baraita 2: **Come and learn. If two people live in a courtyard and one of them wishes to open a business as (1) a mohel, (2) a blood-letter, (3) a weaver or (4) a teacher of children, the other can prevent him!**

Rava: This, again, refers to a teacher of OVEID KOKHAVIM (pagan children). If the text doesn't specifically say "Torah," it wasn't intended to include Torah.

Narrator: Then the rabbi who is arguing with Rava quotes a third Baraita.

Baraita 3: **Come and learn. If a person has a room in a courtyard, he must not rent it to (1) a mohel, (2) a blood-letter, (3) a weaver, (4) a SOFER or (5) a non-Jewish teacher.**

Amora 2: This time, you have to admit that I gotcha! Here we've got a SOFER that says "Torah" teacher, and we have non-Jewish teacher as a different category. So your Hebrew school is clearly excluded, too!

Rashi: What does SOFER mean in this context? SOFER usually means "scribe," but here it refers to a "Jewish teacher."

Tosafot: Wrong! Here the word SOFER means a "town scribe" who would have a large number of visitors coming to him.

Rabbi Gershom[20]: Wrong! Here the word is actually is SAPAR, a "barber," not a SOFER.

Rava: In this BARAITA, SOFER actually means the head teacher of a town, the one who supervises all the others. So this does nothing to prove that classes can't be held in a courtyard; it only prohibits faculty meetings. The noise of teachers coming and going isn't covered in the zoning exemption.

Scene 5: A Tangent—Five Thoughts about Jewish Teaching

Narrator: Before we get back to our Mishnah and resolve the courtyard zoning question, the Gemara is going to spend a little while doing a "film tribute" to Yehoshua ben Gamla by presenting five more teaching tips from Rava. In the process of this "teaching tangent" we learn about a principle called KIN'AT SOFRIM, which means "THE

[17]**A BARAITA** is a chunk of legal material from the period of the Mishnah that wasn't included in the redaction of that document. A BARAITA is considered to be an authoritative legal precedent from an earlier period.

[18]**THE RASHBA.** Rabbi Shlomo ben Avraham Aderet. 1235–1310. Spanish Talmudic commentator and legal authority. He was the chief rabbi of Barcelona. Among his teachers were Ramban and Rabbenu Yona; among his students, the Rivta.

[19]**TANNA.** Technical term for rabbis of the mishnaic era. It literally means "teachers" or "repeaters."

[20]**RABBI GERSHOM ME'OR HA-GOLAH,** "the Light of the Diaspora." French/German Talmudic scholar. 960–1040. Rabbi Gershom ran a school in Mainz, Germany, and was the author of many famous *takkanot* (legal decisions), the most famous of which are his _herem_ (ban) against bigamy and a ruling forbidding the unauthorized reading of private letters.

JEALOUSY OF TEACHERS." That phrase will be the key to this whole SUGIA (conversation).

Rava: [TIP 1] According to the ruling of Yehoshua ben Gamla, children should not be regularly made to attend school in another town, but they can be made to attend school in another synagogue in the same town. However, if the other synagogue is across a river, we cannot make them attend and must hire a teacher for them who can teach them in their part of the town. But if there is a bridge across the river and they can safely get to class, we can make them attend. But if the bridge is only a plank, we cannot make them attend.

Rashi: Even if there is only one child, the town must still hire him a teacher.

Tosafot: Wrong. Unless there is a minimum of twenty-five children, a group, there is no need to hire a teacher.

Rava: [TIP 2] The maximum number of students who are to be assigned to one teacher is twenty-five. If there are fifty, we appoint two teachers. If there are forty, we appoint an assistant at the expense of the town.

Rashi: What is a teaching assistant? It is someone who hears the lesson from the teacher with the students and repeats it to them until they know it for themselves.

Rabbenu Yonah[21]: The community must pay the assistant directly and not deduct the assistant's wage from the teacher's salary.

Rava: [TIP 3] If there is a teacher who teaches reasonably well and there is a second teacher who can cover much more material accurately in the same time, we do not replace the first with the second, because without competition the second may grow lazy.

Rabbi Dimi[22]: Wrong! You do appoint the new teacher. He would exert himself even more because "THE JEALOUSY OF TEACHERS INCREASES WISDOM."

Rava: [TIP 4] If there are two teachers and one teaches quickly but his students make mistakes, and the other teaches slowly but without his students making mistakes, we appoint the faster teacher whose students make mistakes because mistakes correct themselves in time.

R. Dimi: Wrong! We appoint the one who teaches more slowly but who makes sure that there are no mistakes.

The jealousy of teachers increases wisdom.

Scene 6: A Tangent within a Tangent within a Tangent—
The Story of Yoav's Teacher

Narrator: Rabbi Dimi's argument with Rava takes us off into a tangent within a tangent. To prove his point, he tells us a midrashic story about King David and his general, Yoav.

R. Dimi: We learn this in the Bible, 1 Kings 11.16

Torah: כִּי־שֵׁשֶׁת חֳדָשִׁים יָשַׁב־שָׁם יוֹאָב וְכָל־יִשְׂרָאֵל עַד־הִכְרִית כָּל־זָכָר בֶּאֱדוֹם

For Yoav and all Israel stayed there six months until he had cut off every male in Edom.

R. Dimi: The females, however, he spared. When Yoav came before King David, David said to him:

David[23]: Why did you only kill the male Edomites?

Narrator: We are now leaving AMUD 21a and entering AMUD 21b.

Yoav[24]: Because it is written in Deuteronomy 25.19,

תִּמְחֶה אֶת־זֵכֶר עֲמָלֵק "You shall blot out [ZAKHAR AMALEK] all the men of Amalek."

David: But the Torah actually says:

Torah: תִּמְחֶה אֶת־זֵכֶר עֲמָלֵק "You shall blot out [ZEYKHER AMALEK], all the memory of Amalek."

Rashi: Amalek is the nation that is very embodiment of evil on earth. Neither God's name nor God's empire can be complete until the seed of Amalek is wiped off of the earth (cf: Exodus 17:16).

Yoav: I was taught that the word was זָכָר [ZAKHAR].

R. Dimi: Yoav then went and saw his teacher. He asked him:

Yoav: How did you teach me to read this verse?

Teacher[25]: זֵכֶר [ZEIKHER].

Tosafot: Dimi's point is that mistakes learned in childhood remain throughout life. He holds the teacher responsible for Yoav having learned it incorrectly. even though the teacher taught it correctly.

[21]**RABBENU YONAH.** Yonah ben Avraham Gerondi. 1200–1263. Spanish ethicist and Talmudic commentator. Yonah's teacher started a campaign against Maimonides' writings, and Yonah joined in. In the end Maimonides' books were burned by the Inquisition. A few years later, in the same square, the Talmud was burned. Yonah took this as divine retribution. He repented. Yonah was famous not only as a scholar but as a voice against immorality.

[22]**RABBI DIMI FROM NEHARDEA.** Babylonian Amora. Head of the academy in Pumbedita 385–388. Two of his most famous appearances in the Talmud are in this SUGIA (conversation). One of his most famous teachings was: "The giving of hospitality is more important than getting to the house of study early" (Shab. 127a).

[23]**KING DAVID.** The second King of Israel. 1010–970 B.C.E. When Saul and Jonathan died in battle, David assumed the throne. The assassination of a rival king, Ishbosheth, in the north allowed David to be crowned king of a united kingdom. With the capture of Jerusalem, he moved his capital there and planned the construction of a temple. However, God declared David's successor as the future builder, "Who will build My 'house.'" His musical skill was legendary. Many psalms were attributed to him. Most of the narrative that recounts David's decline is omitted from the Book of Chronicles.

[24]**YOAV.** One of King David's generals.

[25]**YOAV'S TEACHER.** A character invented by the Gemara.

R. Dimi: Then Yoav took out his sword and threatened to kill his teacher.

Teacher: Why do you do this?

Yoav: Because it is written in Jeremiah[26] 48.10:

אָרוּר עֹשֶׂה מְלֶאכֶת יהוה רְמִיָּה

Torah: Cursed be the one who does the work of the Eternal negligently.

Teacher: Don't kill me. Be satisfied that I am cursed.

Yoav: It also says in that verse:

וְאָרוּר מֹנֵעַ חַרְבּוֹ מִדָּם

Torah: Cursed be the one who keeps his sword back from blood.

R. Dimi: One report says he did kill him. Another report says he didn't.

Scene 7: A Last Thought about Jewish Teaching

Narrator: We step back from the tangent within the tangent and return to the original tangent with Rava's fifth tip about Jewish teaching. This one echoes the tangent by discussing professional liability.

Rava: [TIP 5] A teacher of young children, a vine-keeper, a SHOHET, a blood-letter and a SOFER are all liable to immediate dismissal.

The general principle is that anyone whose mistakes cannot be corrected is subject to immediate dismissal if a mistake is made.

Rashi: This is a person who tends another person's vineyard, usually for half of the crop.

Narrator: We have reached the end of this tangent. And without needing to say more, this whole phase of the argument is over. By the lack of other arguments, the Gemara agrees that Rava's opinion that the noise of children means the noise of children studying Torah is what OUR MISHNAH is protecting. No one can block it.

[26] **JEREMIAH:** Prophet. 628–586 B.C.E. He preached in Jerusalem under King Josiah and his successors. His message indicts his contemporaries for social injustice and religious apostasy. Jeremiah realistically opposed resistance to Babylon, and his insistence on speaking difficult truths landed him in prison and the stocks. When Jerusalem fell to Babylon (586 B.C.E.), Jeremiah was allowed to stay with the Jews who remained, who later took him to Egypt.

INTERMISSION

Talmud texts do not really have intermissions, but this is a halfway point in this passage. We have reached one set of conclusions, and now we are moving onto a new level. So far we have learned:

- People have a right to "privacy" in their living space—even when they have to share it with neighbors.
- Jewish education has a special priority in Jewish life.
- Competition can be a good thing.

In the second half of this passage we are going to explore:

- The limits on "fair" competition.
- The nature of a "neighborhood."
- The dark side of competition—when it causes harm rather than improvement.

Before we move into the second act, it will be easier if we understand a couple of new technical terms and gain a couple of insights.

Mavoi

A **MAVOI** is an alley off of which branch several HATZEROT (courtyards). This MAVOI is a corridor between the HATZER and the street (RESHUT ha-RABIM/public space). A MAVOI is both physically and legally halfway between a street and a courtyard. One is allowed to carry objects on Shabbat in a HATZER, but one is not allowed to do so in RESHUT ha-RABIM/ public space. If a MAVOI has a crossbeam that separates it from the street, one can carry in it on Shabbat.

Often, in mishnaic times, a house would have its own courtyard, while many such houses would share a single MAVOI as common space.

Previously in the discussion of OUR MISHNAH we have learned that if you live in one HATZER (courtyard) you cannot prevent someone from opening up a business in another HATZER. Now the Gemara is asking, What about two HATZEROT (courtyards) in the same MAVOI?

Ḥazakah

Like the questions of TENURE for teachers discussed previously, this passage considers extending the idea of ḤAZAKAH to give protection through "zoning" to established business, in a given community.

The rabbis assume that our Mishnah has already granted protection to businesses set up in a ḤATZER. Now it wants to know if the same principle can be extended to a MAVOI.

Hasagat Gevul

In the introduction (page 6) we saw the idea of HASAGAT GEVUL, "invading a boundary." This is a term used for, among other things, encroaching on the space of another business or profession. While that was a background idea in the "first act," suggesting that one business can keep another business out of a ḤATZER by complaining about added "busy-ness," in this half of the SUGIA, our "second act," it will become the central question.

Kinat Sofrim

At the end of the first act we met the concept of KIN'AT SOFRIM (the jealousy of SOFRIM/teachers). We learned that there are times when competition makes things better. We have already learned that "the jealousy of teachers increases wisdom." Now we are going to apply the same principles to business—asking what competition is fair and what competitive acts are unfair.

Full Circle

Most of the "second act" will address business issues. At the end of this SUGIA (conversation) we will come back to a story about competition among teachers. We will see it get out of hand—and learn about the "dark side" of jealously and competition.

<u>H</u>EVRUTA LEARNING:
Yored L'Tokh Umanut <u>H</u>aveiro

YORED L'TOKH UMANUT <u>H</u>AVEIRO is a rabbinic term that literally means "going into your friend's profession" but carries the understanding that it is wrong "to take away another person's livelihood through economic competition." This term is not used in this passage (though it is alluded to). The concept is very much in the forefront of the minds of the commentators as they work through and unpack the material that follows. Read the following sources and see if you can (a) understand the meaning of this rabbinic value, and (b) get a sense of the disagreement over its application.

Text 1: Sanhedrin 81a

Narrator: Rabbi A<u>h</u>a bar <u>H</u>anina[27] taught:

R. A<u>h</u>a: One who goes competitively into a neighbor's business/profession and destroys that neighbor's livelihood is like a person who committed adultery.

Text 2: Makkot 24a

Narrator: David came and reduced being a righteous person to eleven principles. (One of them was:)

Torah: One who does not do evil to neighbors (Psalm 15.3).

Amora: This means one who does not go into unfair competition against neighbors.

Gris: The rabbis credit King David with the authorship of the Psalms. Everything said in them is seen as part of his teaching.

Text 3: Kiddushin 59a

Narrator: Rabbi Gidal[28] was negotiating to buy a field when Rabbi Abba[29] went and bought it. Thereupon Rabbi Gidal went and complained about him to Rabbi Zera[30]. Rabbi Zera then went in turn and complained to Yitz<u>h</u>ak Nappaha[31].

Yitz<u>h</u>ak said to him

Yitz<u>h</u>ak: Wait until he comes up to us for the Festival.

[27]**RABBI A<u>H</u>A BAR <u>H</u>ANINA:** Palestinian Amora. c. 300 c.e. He came from Lydda and moved to Galilee. In Tiberias he studied under Rabbi Assi. Some scholars maintain that he visited Babylonia and studied under Rav Huna.

[28]**RABBI GIDAL:** A Babylonian Amora. He was a student of Rav. Best lesson: "When we quote something in the name of its original teacher, we should imagine that teacher standing before us." (JT Shabbat 1.2)

[29]**RABBI ABBA:** A Babylonian Amora who went to *Eretz Yisrael*. He probably knew Rav and Samuel, the founders of rabbinic learning in Babylonia, in his youth, but he was a disciple of Rav Huna and Rav Yehudah. He has a connection to Rabbi Zera. Abba's teachings are found in both the Babylonian and Palestinian Talmuds, as well as in the Midrash.

[30]**RABBI ZERA:** A Babylonian Amora who later moved to *Eretz Yisrael*. c. 300. He studied in the academy of Sura under Huna and in Pumbedita under Yehudah ben Ye<u>h</u>ezkeyl. In *Eretz Yisrael* he attended the school of Yo<u>h</u>anan in Tiberias.

[31]**YITZ<u>H</u>AK NAPPAHA:** Palestinian Amora. Yitz<u>h</u>ak studied under Rabbi Yo<u>h</u>anan in Tiberias.

Narrator:	When he came up he met and asked
Yitzhak:	If a poor man is examining a cake to buy or beg for it and another comes and takes it away from him, what then?
Narrator:	Rabbi Abba answered:
Rabbi Abba:	He is called a wicked man.
Yitzhak:	Then why did you act in the same manner?
Narrator:	He said:
Rabbi Abba:	I did not know that he was negotiating for it.
Yitzhak:	Then let him have it now.
Rabbi Abba:	I will not sell it to him because it is the first field I have ever bought. This is not a good omen. But if he wants it as a gift, let him take it.
Narrator:	Rabbi Giddal would not take possession of the field, because it is written:
Torah:	But one who hates gifts shall live (Proverbs 15.27).
Narrator:	Nor would Rabbi Abba, because Rabbi Giddal had negotiated for it. Neither one of them took possession of it. After this it was called "the rabbis' field."
Maharshal:	In the case of the poor person who was looking for a piece of cake, the Rokeah taught.
Rokeah[32]:	One who encroaches competitively on a neighbor's livelihood is violating the mitzvah of:
Torah:	Cursed be anyone who moves a neighbor's boundary marker (Deuteronomy 27.17).
Rokeah:	The moving of boundaries also includes removing the boundaries of fair business practice (She'elot u'Teshuvot Maharshal #89).
Hatam Sofer[33]:	There is a distinction between competition that will decrease the income of the original businessperson and new competition that will eliminate that income completely. Rashi would agree that if the new store makes it nearly impossible for the old store to succeed, then it would be forbidden. The Talmud never sanctioned putting another store owner out of business (H. M. 79).

Avir Ya'akov[34]: The Hatam Sofer is wrong. One is technically permitted to put another person out of business. When David listed his eleven "Principles of Righteousness" he was setting a standard for a righteous person. It is meritorious not to, but it cannot be prohibited (Teshuvot 42).

Text 4: Rama, Shulḥan Arukh, Hoshen Mishpat 156

Rama: One businessperson may not prevent a second businessperson from going into competition by saying "You are interfering with my livelihood."

Text 5: Ḥavot Ya'ir (Responsa, Siman #42)

Havot Yair[35]: It is permitted to compete with a neighbor unless you are a citizen of a different town who does not pay taxes to the local government... This is the custom among all Jewish communities.

[32]**ROKEAH.** Rabbi Elazar Rokeaḥ of Worms. German rabbinical scholar. 1165–1238. He was one of the Ḥasidei Ashkenaz, a group of German pietists. His major work was *Sefer ha-Rokeaḥ*, a guide to ethics and halakhah. The Ramban was one of his students.

[33]**HATAM SOFER.** Rav Moshe Sofer (Schreiber). German legal scholar. 1763–1840. His main work includes a collection of responsa encompassing several volumes and a commentary to the *Shulḥan Arukh*.

[34]**AVIR YA'AKOV.** Work by Jacob Samson Shabbetai Sinigaglia of Ancora, Italy. d. 1840.

[35]**HAVOT YA'IR.** A collection of responsa by Rabbi Yair Hayyim Bachrach. Worms, Germany. 1638–1702.

ACT II: Competitive Businesses & Rival Teachers

Gris: Now we are to expand our conversation about competition beyond a single HATZER to a MAVOI. Three opinions will be stated. Rabbi Huna is first.

Scene 1: The First Opinion

STONE OIL PRESS

Narrator: Rav Huna said:

R. Huna[36]: If a person who lives in a MAVOI system sets up a commercial mill and later another person who lives in the same MAVOI system (but not in the same HATZER) wants to set up a competitive mill, the first person has the right to stop the second. The first miller can say:

Miller: You are cutting off my livelihood.

Gris: This "FIRST OPINION" is a statement of the value of YORED L'TOKH UMANUT HAVEIRO (cutting off my livelihood).

Rashi: Why could a mill be forbidden? Is it manufacture? The mill that normally would be considered "manufacture" (and had to be permitted in a courtyard) is only forbidden if it is a "commercial" mill and outside customers bring their grain to it.

Ramban: A member of the MAVOI association who has a door that opens onto the MAVOI may set up a craft area outside of his home. No other resident can object on the grounds that this will lengthen the route that he or she travels.

Amora 1: We have a contradiction. This opinion of Rav Huna seems to conflict with Rava's previous statement. He said [in the first part of our SUGIA]:

Gris: We've saved you flipping back a number of pages; here is a restatement of that passage.

Rava: If you were right and this is what the Mishnah meant, it would have directly said, "It is permitted to open a store in another courtyard, and only the people who live in that courtyard can block it."

28

Narrator: If Rava is right (and only courtyard residents have a vote), then Rav Huna is wrong. The core question is: "Is a MAVOI more like a street (where open competition is allowed) or more like a courtyard (where competition can be restricted?)"

Scene 2: The Second Opinion

Gris: While the following "proof text" supports Rav Huna's opinion, it is actually based on different reasoning. Rav Huna has argued "interference with income." This BARAITA introduces the idea of HASAGAT GEVUL—the violation of boundaries.

Amora 1: Rav Huna's view that a MAVOI is legally like a courtyard is supported by the following BARAITA:

Baraita: **Other fishermen's nets must be kept away from the hiding spot of a fish that has already been spotted by another fisherman. They must be kept as far away as the distance that a fish normally swims, just under three miles.**

FISHERMAN
THROWING NET INTO
WATER

Amora 1: Even though the fish are not yet in the net, they are essentially "already caught." By fishing in the first fisherman's "zone" you are essentially stealing the fish he is certain to catch. The same is true of a competitive business in the same MAVOI.

Gris: This second opinion is a direct statement of HASAGAT GEVUL— business boundaries. It reaches the same conclusion but argues differently.

Scene 3: A Sidebar in the Tosafot

Gris: The discussion that follows involves Rabbenu Tam (one of the TOSAFOT) and Rashbam (a later Talmudic commentator). It centers on the issue of two people who try to acquire a HEFKER object. HEFKER is a technical term for an "unowned" or "abandoned" object that is ready for acquisition. When a person picks up a HEFKER object, that person automatically owns it.

Rabbenu Tam[37]: [a] In a case where one person is looking to find and acquire a HEFKER (an ownerless) object and another person finds and acquires it first, this is not an act of wickedness.

[b] However, if a poor person is searching through that which has been thrown out in order to find a cake and another comes

[36]**RABBI HUNA.** A Babylonian Amora who was the head of the yeshiva in Suram, the successor to Rav. He was born in 216 C.E. and died in 296. He was a poor man who worked as a farmer. Later in life he amassed wealth. He shared his wealth with his workers and was famous for helping the poor.

[37]**RABBENU TAM.** Jacob ben Meir Tam. French Talmudic scholar. 1100–1171. Rabbenu Tam was the grandson of Rashi and the son of Meir ben Shmuel, Rashi's son-in-law. His teachers included his father and his brother Shmuel. During the Second Crusade Rabbenu was attacked by Crusaders and was miraculously saved from death. His work formed the backbone of the *Tosafot* on the Babylonian Talmud.

and takes a cake from that same area, it is an act of wickedness (because the person who came and took the cake had more than enough other places to look).

[c] In the same way, the second fisherman (even though the fish is HEFKER/ownerless) is doing something wrong to the first fisherman because there are other places for the second fisherman to put down his nets.

[d] Consider this case. One person (1) paid money to purchase a field but had not completed the rest of the legal arrangements to take possession. Before those conditions were completed another person (2) came and completed the transaction and acquired the field. The second person has done nothing wrong, because in this case there is no other easy place for him to look for other free land.

Rashbam[38]: Wrong! It is just like the net. It is "poaching" from a business deal another person was in the process of consummating.

Gris: These examples are drawn from Kiddushin 59a, a text we looked at in the "Intermission." Now the Talmud continues looking into this issue.

Scene 4: Analysis of Rav Huna's Argument

Amora 2: Wrong! THE CASE OF THE FISH is different from THE CASE OF THE MILL because fish actively go out and look for food. Once they have locked in on it, they will always go to it. But such is not the case with customers in a MAVOI. If they don't like the service, they will go elsewhere.

Rashi: The new merchant can say to the established one, "Whoever wants to go to you will go to you, and whoever wants to go to me will go to me."

Narrator: Ravina said to Rava:

Ravina[39]: Does this mean that by refusing to allow one merchant to take the customers of another, Rav Huna uses the same principle as did Rabbi Judah in a dispute he had with the rest of the TANNA'IM?

Gris: Here is that dispute.

Narrator: We have learned that Rabbi Judah argued in a Mishnah (Bava Metzia 60a):

R. Yehudah[40]: A shopkeeper should not give presents of parched corn and nuts to children because these gifts condition them to return to his store.

Rashi: Honey-roasted nuts were like candy. When the child was sent to the store, she or he would always go to the store that served treats.

Mishnah: But the rabbis permit this behavior.

R. Steinsaltz[41]: In the Mishnah, when a given Tanna's opinion is stated first and then followed by an anonymous (or majority) opinion, the Halakhah follows the anonymous opinion.

Narrator: The PROBLEM here is that Rav Huna seems to be backing the losing side. Just as the rabbis permitted competition among shopkeepers who gave out snacks, competition should be allowed here. Rabbi Huna should know his Mishnah better than to be arguing an opinion that has already been rejected.

Amora 1: But there is another way to look at this. In fact, you can argue that Rav Huna agrees with the other TANNA'IM. Rabbi Yehudah lost that argument. Why is Rav Huna following him? The TANNA'IM reasoned that if another shopkeeper complained about gifts given by the first shopkeeper, he was correct in saying to him:

Shopkeeper 1: Just as I give away almonds, you can give away walnuts.

Ritva: This explanation applies to a situation when both stores are already established; it is fair for them to compete. It does not speak to the question of new competition.

Rambam[42]: It is reasonable for a store owner to distribute nuts or candy to children to encourage business. It is also reasonable to lower prices. This is not G'NAVAT DAT ("stealing the mind" or "deceit").

Amora 1: But in the case Rav Huna has raised about a new merchant who moves into the territory of an established business in a courtyard, even the TANNA'IM concede that the original miller can say to the newcomer

Shopkeeper 1: You are cutting off my livelihood.

Narrator: And thereby prevent him from setting up his business in that courtyard. So far, Rabbi Huna's opinion stands because it has support from the TANNA'IM.

31

[38]**RASHBAM:** Rabbi Shmuel ben Meir. French Talmudic scholar. 1085–1174. He was a grandson of Rashi, and his Torah commentary is famous for its emphasis on the plain meaning of the text. He studied with Rashi and was the the teacher of his brother, Rabbenu Tam.

[39]**RAVINA:** A Babylonian Amora. He died in 420. He was a student of Yoseph ben Hama and played an important role in editing the Talmud.

[40]**RABBI YEHUDAH (BEN YEHEZKEYL).** Babylonian Amora. 220–299. Nicknamed "the sharp one" or the "big tooth." He was tall and earned his living selling wine. Rabbi Yehudah founded the academy in Pumbedita in 259. He studied with Rav but tended to agree with Shmuel. He was a peer of Rav Huna. In 297 he was chosen to head the leading academy, Sura.

[41]**RABBI ADIN STEINSALTZ:** Israeli Talmudic scholar: b. 1937. He founded the Israel Institute for Talmudic Publications, and since then has been working on a monumental project of translating and reinterpreting the Talmud. This new edition of the Talmud has made the Talmud accessible to tens of thousands of Hebrew speakers. In 1989 he began producing an English edition of this Talmud. In 1994 the first two volumes of the Steinsaltz Talmud appeared in French, and the first volume in Russian, appeared.

[42]**RAMBAM:** Rabbi Moshe ben Maimon (Maimonides). Spanish doctor, philosopher and legal scholar. 1135–1204. Born in Cordova, Spain, he moved to Morocco and finally to Egypt. Included in his works are the *Mishneh Torah*, a legal work that codifies all of the laws found throughout the Talmud; *Sefer HaMitzvot*, which lists and explains the 613 commandments; and the *Moreh Nevuhim*, a philosophical treatise.

Scene 5: An Objection

Narrator: Another rabbi, not named, objected to Rav Huna's ruling that one neighbor can stop another neighbor from setting up a competitive mill in a MAVOI.

Amora 1: Rabbi Huna is wrong. Look at this BARAITA:

Baraita: **A person can open a store next to another person's store, or a bathhouse next to another person's bathhouse, and the owner of the first store or bath cannot object. If he complains, the owner of the new business can tell him:**

New Owner: **I do what I like on my property, and you do what you like on your property.**

Amora 1: In other words, contrary to Rav Huna, this Baraita says fair competition is fair competition and can't be stopped.

Narrator: This second opinion is also established with Tana'itic proof. Now we have a problem, because we have two different versions of "what God has told us to do." This contradiction poses a problem.

Scene 6: Looking at Another Objection

Amora 1: Then take a look at this Baraita. It provides another old version of this conversation:

Baraita: **The residents of a MAVOI can block one another from renting their space to a competitive tailor, tanner, teacher, or any other craftsperson, but they cannot block another resident from setting up her/his own competitive business.**

Rabban Shimon ben Gamliel[43]**:** **Wrong, they may block each other.**

Gris: Later the discussion will struggle with the meaning of "neighbor." Is it anyone from the MAVOI or anyone from the town?

Tosafot: We already know that residents cannot block a Torah teacher from holding class in a HATZER (courtyard). Logically, the same holds true for a MAVOI (shared alley), where the connection is less direct. Therefore, the teacher here must be a teacher of non-Jewish subjects.

Narrator: The anonymous voice in this BARAITA argues that there is a difference between a neighbor and an outsider who wants to go into competition with an existing business. Rabban Shimon ben Gamliel argues that there is no difference.

Scene 7: Act Three: The Third Opinion

Gris: In response to this discussion, Rabbi Huna Berei d'Rabbi Yehoshua brings in the third opinion.

R. Huna Bd'RY[44]: It is quite clear to me that Rabban Shimon Ben Gamliel is wrong. Even though the resident of one town can prevent the resident of another town from coming into his town and setting up a competitive business, this doesn't apply if the outsider pays taxes to this new town.

Even though a town businessperson can prevent an outsider from going into competition, the resident of a MAVOI cannot block another resident of the same MAVOI from setting up a competitive business.

Gris: This is a clear application of the BARAITA's statement, "But they cannot block a neighbor from setting up her/his own competitive business." The rabbis' assumption: you can block a non-neighbor.

Tosafot: The members of a MAVOI can prevent a person from setting up shop in their MAVOI, but they cannot prevent that person from setting up shop elsewhere in the city if the person has paid his taxes.

Rabbenu Yona: This is true if the person has paid even a fraction of the local taxes. But a town need not accept tax payments from everyone who wants to set up a business.

R. Huna Bd'RY: But here is the question. If we follow the law according to the BARAITA, can the resident of a MAVOI block another resident of that MAVOI (from a different HATZER) from setting up a competitive business in his own HATZER?

When the BARAITA argues that the resident of a HATZER cannot block a "neighbor," how big is the neighborhood: a HATZER, a MAVOI, or the whole town?

33

[43]**RABBAN SHIMON BEN GAMLIEL.** Head of the Sanhedrin in *Eretz Yisrael* in the first century during the time of the destruction of the Temple.

[44]**RABBI HUNA BEREI RABBI YEHOSHUA.** Babylonian Amora. d. 410. He was a student of both Rava and Abaye and the business partner of Rav Papa. They sold beer. He was the number two at the academy in Naresh. He is the Talmudic source for the kippah (Shab. 118b).

Rashi: It is clear that members of a MAVOI cannot stop another member of the same MAVOI from entering a business or profession. What Rabbi Huna Berei d/Rabbi Yehoshua is asking is, "Can he stop the member of an adjoining courtyard from going into a business?" Is he/she considered a neighbor?

Narrator: TEY-KU—we just don't know.

Narrator: In modern Hebrew, a TEY-KU is a "tie." It is sometimes said that it stands for TISHBI YA' ANEH al KUSHIOT V'SH'EILOT—"When Elijah the prophet returns with the Messiah, all such questions and problems will be solved."

Gris: Let's review what we have learned (the framework for this analysis is found in the Shottenstein Edition of the Talmud):

[1] A non-resident can be blocked from setting up a competitive business within a town.

[2] A non-resident who is a taxpayer in a given town cannot be blocked from setting up a competitive business in that town, but can be blocked from setting it up in a given MAVOI where a previously established business exists.

[3] A town resident may always open up a competitive business. What is unclear is whether or not he can be blocked from doing so in a specific MAVOI where such a business already exists.

[4] It is also unclear whether the resident of a given MAVOI can open a competitive business within that MAVOI.

Later Opinions

Tosafot: Rabbi Huna berai d'Rabbi Yehoshua is right—one neighbor cannot prevent another neighbor from going into competition.

The Rosh[45]: Rav Huna berei d'Rabbi Yehoshua is correct because he was backed by the majority of the rabbis (on Bava Batra 12).

Rama: One businessperson may not prevent a second businessperson from going into competition by saying, "You are interfering with my livelihood" (Bet Yosef, Shulhan Arukh H. M. 156).

Havot Ya'ir: It is permitted to compete with a neighbor unless you are a citizen of a different town who does not pay taxes to the local government... this is the custom among all Jewish communities (T'shuvot Havot Ya'ir 42).

Mordechai[46]: If a person has a store at the end of a dead-end alley and another person wants to come along and open a store near to the mouth of that alley, it seems to me that original store owner can block the new store, just as Rav Huna ruled (Mordechai, Shekheinim 6).

Hatam Sofer: Rav Huna's opinion is not rejected by the rabbis. If a new store will cause an existing shop some financial loss (Hulshat Haiytei), competition cannot be blocked. But if the new store will threaten the existence of the old store (Pisuk Haiytei), based on the principle of YORED L'TOKH UMANUT HAVEIRO—competing with one's neighbor's living—it can be blocked. Rabbi Huna berai d'Rabbi Yehoshua was only speaking of competition that does not threaten the existence of the first store owner (Responsa Hoshen Mishpat 71).

Rabbi Moshe Feinstein: Loss of a living is not defined as drastically as loss of a home or inability to put food on the table, but as taking away as much as an average person of that socioeconomic class would consider "financial ruin" (Teshuvot Iggerot Moshe, Hoshen Mishpat).

Divrei Hayyim[47]: Today there is no alley that is reserved for its neighbor, and the entire city and its alleys are one, and everyone is equal (She'elot u'Tshuvot Divrei Hayyim, Hoshen Mishpat, Siman 35).

Piskei Din Rabbaniyim[48]: A modern MAKOLET, a neighborhood grocery store, in an Israeli SHIKKUN, neighborhood, is the equivalent of a mill set up in a dead-end MAVOI and should be protected (6.3).

Gris: We will discuss these further when we return to the opening case studies in the concluding essay.

Scene 8: Five "Free Trade" Zoning Variance Cases

Case One

Narrator: Now we are going to find within education an exception to this rule about competition within a MAVOI.

Rav Yosef said:

R. Yosef[49]: In fact, in another lesson that Rabbi Huna taught, he seemed to agree that fair competition among neighbors can't be limited. In applying the same principle to education, he said:

[45]**THE ROSH.** Rav Asher ben Yehiel. b. 1250 in Germany d. 1327 in Spain. He was a student of Maharam MiRutenberg. Because of anti-Semitism he fled to Spain in 1303, where he became the Rabbi of Toledo. He is best known for his massive halakhic commentary to the Talmud.

[46]**MORDECHAI.** Mordechai ben Hillel, who was the son-in-law of Rav Yehiel of Paris. German Talmudic scholar. Late 1200s. His main work is known simply as Mordechai, and it is a collection of laws arranged according to the order of the Talmud. He and his entire family were killed in the Rindfleisch massacres in 1298.

[47]**DIVREI HAYYIM.** The name of two different books written by Rabbi Hayyim ben Leivush (1793–1876). He was a Hasidic rabbi who founded a dynasty in Zanz.

[48]**PISKEI DIN RABBANIYIM.** A collection of legal decisions by modern Israeli religious courts.

[49]**RABBI YOSEF (BAR HIYYAH).** Babylonian Amora. 270–333. He was a friend of Rabbah bar Nahmani, with whom he debated regularly. He was the teacher of Rava and Abaye. His nickname was "Sinai" because of his amazing Torah knowledge. In 330 he became the Rosh Yeshiva in Pumbedita.

R. Huna: A teacher cannot prevent another teacher from setting up a competitive class in the same MAVOI, because of a reason already mentioned: THE JEALOUSY OF TEACHERS INCREASES WISDOM.

Yosef Caro[50]: Even if the competitive teacher comes from another town (_Hoshen Mishpat_ 156.6).

Case Two

Narrator: Here is another exception.

Rav Naḥman bar Rav Yitzḥak[51] said:

R. Naḥman: Rav Huna ben Rav Yehoshua also agrees that fair competition cannot be prevented:

Rav Huna b. RY: Itinerant spice-sellers cannot prevent one another from going to any given town, because as it was taught:

Baraita: **Ezra made a rule for Israel that spice-sellers should go from town to town so that the daughters of Israel would be able to obtain nice things.**

Rashi: Spice-sellers are a euphemism for people who sell makeup.

Gris: This ruling is one of the ten TIKKUNEI EZRA (Ezra's Reforms) that created the process that led to the Talmud.[52]

Amora 1: This ruling, however, only meant that while itinerant spice-sellers are free to go from house to house in a strange town, they are not free to settle there. If, however, the seller is a student, he may settle there. This exception comes from a precedent set by Rava when he allowed Rabbi Josiah and Rabbi Obadiah to set up a permanent shop despite the former ruling. The reason he gave was:

Rava: They were rabbis and they would be disturbed in their studies if they couldn't set up a stand.

Rashi: Even though this isn't the literal interpretation of the law, it does fall within the law. The reasoning is that the effort to peddle from door to door would have distracted them from their studies.

Case Three

Narrator: Here is another ruling restricting competition. It is a place where another exception is made to the ruling that tradesmen can be barred in places where they do not live. This time it is ethical rather than educational reasons that invite the exception.

Amora 1: There once were these basket sellers who brought baskets to Babylon to sell. The townspeople came and asked Ravina to block them from selling their wares.

Ravina: They are foreigners, and while they can be forbidden from setting up stores in the SHUK (marketplace) and selling to citizens, they must be permitted to set up shops in the SHUK and sell to foreigners who are in Babylon.

Rashi: In the SHUK on market day, many of the customers came from outside the city (and were not citizens). We cannot prevent non-citizens from selling to them.

Ravina: In other words, they can sell in the SHUK only on market days, but not on other days. Even on market days they cannot go selling door-to-door to the residents of the city.

Case Four

Narrator: Here is another "business" exemption to this ruling.

Amora 2: There were once wool merchants who brought wool to Pum Nahara. The townspeople tried to block them from selling it. They appealed to Rav Kahana, who said:

R. Kahana[53]: They have a perfect right to stop you from selling your goods here.

Narrator: But they responded:

[50]**RABBI YOSEF CARO (a.k.a. BEIT YOSEF).** Spanish, Turkish, Israeli legal authority. 1488-1575. He taught and later died in Eretz Yisrael. His main work was the Beit Yosef, a commentary on the Tur. This work was then published in digest form as the Shulhan Arukh. Additionally, he wrote a commentary on Mishneh Torah of Maimonides known as the Kesef Mishnah, and a set of responsa.

[51]**RABBI NAHMAN BEN ISAAC.** Babylonian Amora. b. 280. He and Rava were both students of Nahman ben Ya'acov in Nehardea. He moved to Sura and studied with Nahman ben Hisda. After Rava's death his school in Mahuza was merged with the school in Pumbedita. Nahman became the head of that yeshiva.

[52]**TIKKUNEI EZRA.** The Talmud remembers that Ezra was the author of ten TIKKUNIM—repairs, fixes, reforms, changes—to the Jewish tradition. These changes are the beginning of the transformation of Judaism from its biblical expression to the Judaism we now live. (1) Torah is to be read on Shabbat afternoon (in a synagogue). (2) Torah is to be read on Mondays and Thursdays (in a synagogue). (3) Courts should be held on Mondays and Thursdays (and they should use the Torah to "judge between the people"). (4) To get ready for a home Shabbat experience, clothes should be washed on Thursdays. (5) Because it is an aphrodisiac, garlic should be eaten on Fridays (to set up "the double mitzvah"). (6) The housewife should rise early to bake bread. (7) A woman must wear a *sinnar* (a garment to protect modesty). (8) A woman must comb her hair before going to the mikveh. (9) Peddlers (who are selling makeup) must be given an exemption to the rule that non-Jews cannot sell to Jews. (10) Men may have moments when they have to go to the mikveh, too (Bava Kama 82a).

[53]**RAV KAHANA (IV).** Babylonia Amora. He was a student of Rava's and a teacher of Rav Ashi and Rava's son Aha. He was the head of the Yeshiva in Pum Nahara.

Merchants: We have money owing to us here. If we are not allowed to support ourselves by selling until the debt is paid, we will never collect what is owed us.

R. Kahana: If so, you can go and sell only enough to live off until you collect your debts. Then you must go.

EPILOGUE: A Story

Narrator: Here we have a story that combines business rules and educational principles. We are back to the principle of KIN'AT SOFRIM—the jealousy of teachers.

Rabbi Dimi from Nehardea, a newcomer, brought a boatload of figs to sell. The Exilarch (the head of the community) said to Rava:

Exilarch[54]: Go and check out if he is a scholar. If he is a rabbinic student of quality, prevent competitive merchants from selling their goods before he can set up his shop.

Narrator: So Rava said to his student Rav Adda bar Ahavah[55]:

Rava: Go and smell his jar.

Rashi: This means to "test if he is wine or vinegar," and that means "check out his scholarship."

Narrator: So Rav Adda bar Ahavah went and asked Rav Dimi the following question:

R. A.b.A.: If an elephant swallows a willow wood basket and then passes it out as excrement, is it "clean" or "unclean"?

Rashi: To explain: The Torah lists the types of containers that can pick up TUMAH (ritual uncleanliness) (Leviticus 11:32–33, Numbers 31: 20–24). Among them are wooden and reed baskets. However, tools

39

[54]**EXILARCH (Reish Galuta/Head of the Exile).** The title given the head of the Jewish community in Babylonia. This position was hereditary and was held by a descendent of King David.

[55]**RABBI ADDA BAR AHAVAH.** Babylonian Amora. c. 300s. He was a student of Rava. It is said that he used to study each piece of Torah twenty-four times, once for each book in the Bible (Ta'anit 8a). This story is his major appearance in the Talmud.

made of excrement cannot pick up a TUMAH because of rabbinic interpretation (Keilim 10.1 and Menahot 69b). Adda bar Ahavah is asking: After its "journey," what do we consider the "substance" of the basket—is it still willow wood or is it now something else?

Rashba: By the way, the correct answer is that it can still contract TUMAH, because no matter where it has been, unless its physical form is changed, it remains the same object. It is still willow wood.

Narrator: Rav Dimi could not answer. Instead he asked:

R. Dimi: Are you Rava?

Narrator: Rav Adda bar Ahavah tapped his staff on Dimi's shoe and said:

R. A.b.A.: Between me and Rava there is a great difference, but at any rate, I can be your teacher, and that makes Rava the teacher of your teacher.

Narrator: They did not reserve the market for him, and his figs were sold for a loss. He appealed to Rabbi Yosef, saying:

R. Dimi: Rabbi, see how they have treated me?

Narrator: He said to him:

R. Yosef: The One who did not delay to avenge the wrong done to the king of Edom will not hesitate to avenge the wrong done to you, as it is written in Amos, 2.1.

Amos[56]: The Eternal said: "For three sins of Moab, in fact for four, I will not hold back punishment, because God saw to it that the bones of the king of Edom were burned in lime."

Amora 1: Shortly afterwards Rabbi Adda bar Ahavah died.

Narrator: After his death many famous members of the rabbinic community felt responsible for the death. Each of them had his own reason to hate Rabbi Adda bar Ahavah. After his death each of them felt guilty about that hate.

R. Yosef: He was punished because of what he did to me—I cursed him by saying that God would soon avenge Rabbi Dimi.

R. Dimi: He was punished because of what he did to me—he made me lose my figs.

Abaye: He was punished because of what he did to me—he used to say to the students of Rava:

R. A.b.A.: Instead of gnawing at bones in the school of Abaye, why don't you eat fat meat in the school of Rava?

Rava: He was punished because of what he did to me. When he went to the butcher to buy meat, he used to say to the butcher:

R. A.b.A.: Serve me before the servant of Rava because I am above him.

Rashi: Rava was afraid that Rav Adda bar Ahavah was punished for insulting him.

R. Naḥman b. Yitzḥak[57]: Rabbi Adda bar Ahavah was punished because of what he did to me:

Amora 1: Rav Naḥman bar Yitzḥak was the regular giver of the Shabbat sermon. Before each sermon he would go over it with Rav Adda bar Ahavah. Only then would he go and give it. One day Rav Papa[58] and Rav Huna berei d'Rabbi Yehoshua got hold of Rav Adda bar Ahavah because they had missed the final lesson on tractate Brakhot. They asked him:

R. Papa & R. Huna bd'RY: Tell us how Rava discussed the law of the "Last Chapter of Brakhot."

Amora 1: He then gave him a full account of Rava's lesson on "The Tithing of Cattle." Meanwhile, the sun had set and Rav Naḥman was still waiting for Rav Adda bar Ahavah.

Narrator: The rabbis said to him:

Rabbis: Come, it is late. What are you waiting for?

R. Naḥman: I am waiting for the bier of Rav Adda bar Ahavah.

Amora 1: Soon the report came that Rav Adda bar Ahavah was dead.

Amora 2: It is most likely that Rav Naḥman bar Yitzḥak was the cause of his punishment.

Rashi: A curse uttered by a righteous person. even one s/he doesn't really mean. is carried out immediately. In Moed Katan 18a and Bava Metzia 68a. this is compared to the orders of a king to execute someone. which are immediately carried out. even if the king is in error.

[56]**AMOS.** Judean Prophet of the 8th Century B.C.E. c.760. He was born in Tekoa, five miles to the south of Bethlehem, in Judea, but made his major prophecy in Beth El, in Israel, during the rule of King Jeroboam II. His is the oldest book of the literary prophets.

[57]**RAV NAḤMAN BAR YITZḤAK.** Babylonian Amora. d. 356. He was a peer of Rava and a student of Rabbi Naḥman ben Ya'akov. After Rava's death he became the head of the Yeshiva in Mahuza, which moved to Pumbedita.

[58]**RABBI PAPA.** Babylonian Amora. c. 300–375. His teachers included Rava and Abaye. He was a friend of Rabbi Huna berei d'Rabbi Yehoshua and headed the yeshiva at Narash from 352–371. Rabbi Papa started out poor and became wealthy. Two hundred students used to eat as his table.

FINAL THOUGHTS: Today's Applications

Values

Inside this SUGIA we have dealt with a number of Jewish values that are important to carry away with us. These include:

1. **TALMUD TORAH K'NEGED KULAM** (Jewish education is more important than anything): From the notion that Torah learning gets a "zoning variance" we learn both the priority and the special circumstances we should create to enable Jewish learning.

2. **KI MI-TZION TEITZEI TORAH** (From Jerusalem goes forth Torah): From the story of universal Jewish education starting in Jerusalem (even though it didn't work completely) we learn the place that Jerusalem and Israel need to have in the heart and mind of every Jew and every Jewish community.

3. **KIN'AT SOFRIM MARBEH TORAH** (the jealousy of teachers increases wisdom): In this passage we start out learning that competition is good—that both commerce and education are strengthened through competition. But through our consideration of legal cases and the story of Rabbi Dimi and Rabbi Adda bar Ahavah we learn that competition has a shadow and can do harm.

4. **HASAGAT GEVUL** (not infringing on the boundaries of another person's business): The idea of respecting borders and boundaries has a lot of important contexts.

5. **YORED L'TOKH UMANUT <u>H</u>AVEIRO** (going into your friend's profession): This idea of not destroying another person's living sets limitations on the freedom to do everything we want.

Legal Thinking

In the "second act" of this SUGIA we have a discussion of business competition. We get three opinions:

Opinion 1

R. Huna: If a person who lives in a MAVOI sets up a commercial mill and later another person who lives in the same MAVOI (but not in the same <u>H</u>ATZER) wants to set up a competitive mill in the MAVOI, the first person has the right to stop the second. The first miller can say:

Miller: You are cutting off my livelihood.

Gris: This "FIRST OPINION" is a statement of the value of YORED L'TOKH UMANUT HAVEIRO (cutting off livelihood).

Opinion 2

Baraita: Other fishermen's nets must be kept away from the hiding spot of a fish that has already been spotted by another fisherman. They must be kept as far away as the distance that a fish normally swims, just under three miles.

Amora 1: Even though the fish are not yet in the net, they are essentially "already caught." By fishing in the first fisherman's "zone," you are essentially stealing the fish he is certain to catch. The same is true of a competitive business in the same MAVOI.

Gris: This second opinion is a direct statement of HASAGAT GEVUL—business boundaries. It reaches the same conclusion but argues differently than Rabbi Huna.

Opinion 3

R. Huna Bd'RY: Even though a businessperson can prevent an outsider from going into competition, the resident of a MAVOI cannot block another resident of the same MAVOI from setting up a competitive business.

Gris: This is a clear application of the BARAITA's statement, "But they cannot block a neighbor from setting up her/his own competitive business." The rabbis' assumption is that you can block a non-neighbor.

Even though the resolution of this passage is not completely clear in the Gemara, later Talmudic commentators have a need to resolve the conflict between the first two opinions, which limit competition, and Rabbi Huna berai d'Rabbi Yehoshua, who seems to invite unlimited free enterprise.

There are two halakhic (legal) principles that support them: (1) The halakhah (law) usually follows the majority, and (2) the halakhah usually follows the later AMORA. Using these principles we learn:

Tosafot: Rabbi Huna berai d'Rabbi Yehoshua is right—one neighbor cannot prevent another neighbor from going into competition.

The Rosh: Rav Huna berai d'Rabbi Yehoshua is correct because he was backed by the majority of the rabbis (on Bava Batra 21, #12).

> Rama: One businessperson may not prevent a second businessperson from going into competition by saying, "You are interfering with my livelihood" (Bet Yosef, Shulhan Arukh H. M. 156).

However, later voices reason in an interesting way. Rabbi Eliezer ben Yoel ha-Levi, who wrote a lost book called the *Aviasaf*, was quoted in a Talmudic commentary called *Mordechai*, assembled by Rabbi Mordechai ben Hillel (1240–1298). He argues:

> Mordechai: If a person has a store at the end of a dead-end alley and another person wants to come along and open a store near to the mouth of that alley, it seems to me that the original store owner can block the new store—just as Rav Huna ruled (Mordechai, Sheheinim 6).

Yosef Caro, the author of the *Shulhan Arukh,* has big problems with this opinion. He writes:

> Yosef Caro: This argument is nothing more than a restatement of the "fishing net" argument that was rejected by the Gemara.

Later, Rabbi Moshe Sofer, the Hatam Sofer (1763–1839), figures out how to take these two opposing opinions and put them together. Jewish law frequently does exactly that. He figures out how one value (ruling) takes priority in one situation and another value (ruling) takes priority in another situation.

> Hatam Sofer: Rav Huna's opinion is not rejected by the rabbis. If a new store will cause an existing shop some financial loss (Hulshat Hiyteih), competition cannot be blocked. But if the new store will threaten the existence of the old store (Pisuk Hiyteih), based on the principle of YORED L'TOKH UMANUT SHEL HAVEIRO—competing with one's neighbor's living—it can be blocked. Rabbi Huna berai d'Rabbi Yehoshua was only speaking of competition that does not threaten the existence of the first store owner (Responsa Hoshen Mishpat 71).

This set of compromises—this balancing of "free enterprise" with the "protection of livelihood"—becomes the traditional position. Here is how these values were applied to cases at the beginning of this booklet.

The Cases Revisited

We will look at cases two, four and five—the historical cases—first, and then draw from those experiences to look at the other two cases:

4. MISHNEH TORAH COMPETITION: Rabbi Meir of Padua edited a corrected version of Maimonides' *Mishneh Torah* and published it partnership with Aloizi Brogodin of Venice. Marcos Antonio, another publisher from Venice, put out his own competitive edition of the *Mishneh Torah* and sold it at a cheaper price (*Rama, Responsa* 10).

The Rama uses the principle of YORED L'TOKH UMANATO SHEL HAVERO to rule: "Because Rabbi Meir would lose his entire investment in his edition, especially because Marcos Antonio was selling his at a bargain price, the idea of HAZAKAH, the priority of the first person in the market, applies, and the public should not buy the competitive edition."

Later, the Hatam Sofer revisited this case and created the distinction we have looked at between the original owner experiencing a loss and the original owner being put out of business. He echoes the same conclusion, that the new edition should be boycotted.

The Bet Efraim, in a similar case, still holds with the original understanding of Rabbi Huna berei d'Rabbi Yehoshua and permits unbridled competition (*Hoshen Mishpat* 26–7).

2. TAX COLLECTORS: Simon leases the right to collect taxes from a feudal lord. He pays the lord a fee and keeps all of the taxes he collects. Reuben comes and offers the feudal lord a higher fee to collect taxes in the same district. Simon will lose his "job" as the tax collector and his way of earning a living (*She'elot u'Teshuvot Maharshal* # 89).

The Maharshal compares this to the case of the poor man who is looking for a piece of cake (*Kiddushin* 59a). In that case (in the HEVRUTA LEARNING: *Yored L'Tokh Umanut Shel Haveiro*) we learn that someone who searches and takes a piece of cake from the same location is acting in an evil manner. He then connects it to a teaching of the Rokeah (which we have also seen) that this is HASAGAT GEVUL, the removing of the boundaries of a neighbor's business. He forbids it.

Rabbi David Ben Shlomo ibn Abi Zimra, the Radbaz, from Egypt (1479–1573), decided a similar case. He, too, argues that this is "stealing a livelihood" and forbids it (*T'shuvot ha-Radaz, part 4, section 54*).

5. NEW SHUL: Can worshippers leave one synagogue whose survival is at risk to start another that they will like better?

Rabbi Moshe Feinstein solved a case like this. He ruled that old worshippers did not have the right to abandon an old synagogue and new people who moved into this neighborhood did not have the right to compete. He used HASAGAT GEVUL as his principle and based his opinion on the Hatam Sofer's explanation of Rabbi Huna: that one cannot compete with another person if that competition will put the original business (or synagogue) out of business. He does explain that a rabbi can come into the area and teach Torah competitively as long as it does not affect the original rabbi's salary. This would be KIN'AT SOFRIM MARBEH TORAH (the jealousy of teachers increases wisdom).

The Law Committee of the Central Conference of American Rabbis (Reform) dealt with a similar case: "A young rabbi who has settled in the community wishes to create a new congregation. Some individuals in the existing congregations have questioned the need for another congregation and want to know whether his efforts should be permitted and supported."

They respond: "It is clear from some of the earlier sources that multiple synagogues existed in many cities.... However, if the new members are going to separate themselves from an existing congregation, they should not be allowed to form a new congregation *(Pit-hei Teshuvah* to *Shulhan Arukh, Hoshen Mishpat* 162.6; *Magen Avraham* to *Shulhan Arukh, Orekh Hayyim* 154.23). That was modified by later authorities, and permission was granted when the congregants were prone to quarrel if they remained in the same congregation. This allowed multiple congregations with their specific *minhagim* to flourish....

"In the establishment of a new congregation, the rules and procedures of the Union of American Hebrew Congregations and the Codes of Ethics of the Central Conference of American Rabbis should be followed; they provide guidance and will minimize friction with existing congregations" (November 1983).

In other words, diversity is good, divorce is sometimes better than conflict, and we are going to treat this as an administrative issue—not a religious one.

 **3. HIGH FASHION:** There is a street in the city that is the center of women's fashion. Susan wants to become a designer and open her own boutique. She goes to rent a vacant store, but when Valerie, who already has a store in the same building, finds out, she tells her landlord not to rent to another women's clothing store.

Rabbi Moshe D. Tendler and Rav Basri, both contemporary teachers, are quoted in Rabbi Chaim Jachter's *Gray Matter,* self-published 2000, p. 118, permitting competition in a business district when such competition increases traffic for all stores. This would be such a case.

1. CAPITAL BASEBALL: Should the owner of the Baltimore Orioles prevent the Expos from moving to Washington, D.C.?

While we have seen a diversity of responses to the question, most modern legal scholars would follow the Hatam Sofer. He would rule that the competition should be allowed because the new team will most likely not jeopardize the viability of the Orioles. One cannot prevent competition that creates only "some economic loss."

Conclusion

One of the wonderful parts of this story is how two competitive legal arguments from the Talmud grow together into linked values—a progression of solutions. Go for "free enterprise" unless the livelihood of the original store is at risk. Think cake, nets, nuts and dead-end alleys.

FINAL CASES

Here are a few more cases to help you check out your understanding of these principles.

1. MAIN STREET: David has a store on Main Street. His major product line involves clips and ribbons for women to use in their hair. Deborah started pushing a cart to Main Street, setting it up on the sidewalk and selling the same kinds of products at a slightly cheaper price because she has no rent to pay. David also suspects that she pays no license fees or taxes to the city. Now he is thinking of calling the police and asking them to check out her paperwork. His wife argues that what he wants to do is unfair and selfish.

YOU BE THE JUDGE: Is it right for David to call the authorities?

2. COMPETITIVE MARINARA: In an observant neighborhood there is one kosher pizzeria. A competitive kosher pizzeria seeks to move into a vacant storefront about a block away. The original owner goes to the local Bet Din (rabbinical court) and asks for protection.

YOU BE THE JUDGE: What should the court decide?

3. DIRECT SALES: Bob hired Sam as a salesman. Sam worked for Bob for a period of time and met all his clients. Then he stopped working for Bob and took a job with Zack selling the same kind of products to Bob's old customers.

YOU BE THE JUDGE: Can Zack be made to fire Sam? Should HASAGAT GEVUL apply?